1 2 3 4 5

6 7 8 9 10

11 12 13 14 15

16 17 18 19 20

21 22 23 24 25

26 27 28 29 30

Bright Start Right Start
Words

seashell

apple

Jim Bear

tiger

road roller

30

thirty

Scribblers

S

Bright Start Right Start

Betty Bear

A world of words for a brighter start

hair

forehead

eyebrow

eye

face

ear

cheek

nose

mouth

lip

chin

neck

shoulder

arm

hand

ball

elbow

boy

2

Contents

Betty Bear

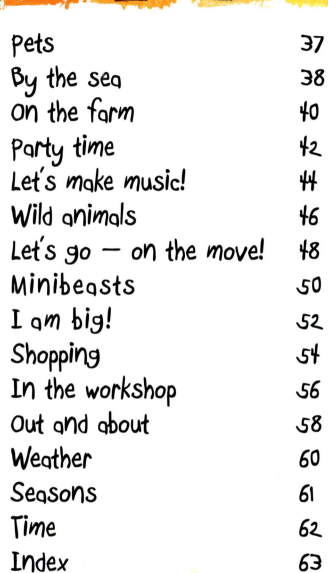

3

How many bears are there?   Can you see Jim Bear?

What colour is the polar bear?

What pattern is the girl's dress?

How to use this book

face

arm

hair

finger

thumb

dress

elbow

Words has been created especially for young children. It will give them a head start in learning vital pre-school skills such as language and number recognition. It includes the words that children are most familiar with by the age of five. Bright, colourful photographs of familiar and unusual objects will help to widen their knowledge of the world around them. Each section has its own theme, to help young children make the connections between words and pictures.

hand

girl

knee

leg

ankle

polar bear

shoes

4

Young children like to look at pictures, and love naming what they see. It is even more fun for them to share a word book with an adult. Start by talking about what is in the picture, and what the object might be used for. Talk about colours and shapes. Look at the scale of the objects – it might be very different on different pages. You can use the questions round the edges of the pages to start a conversation and encourage the child to study the pictures more closely. When they are familiar with the book, show them the index at the back, and explain how it is organised alphabetically.

Children will love searching for the teddy bear on each page.

hair

eyebrow

eye

nose

boy

Jim Bear

shirt

Alphabet — my letters

What words can you spell using the alphabet?

Can you read all of your letters?

A a

B b

C c

D d

E e

Can you find a Q and an R?

F f

G g

H h

I i

J j

K k

L l

M m

6 LETTER

How many letters are in the alphabet?

Can you point to the letter M?

N n

O o

P p

Q q

R r

S s

T t

U u

V v

W w

X x

Y y

Z z

Can you point to the letter G?

LETTERS 7

Numbers

Can you count all the way to 32?

Can you point to 10 and 20?

Can you count to 30?

1 one	2 two	3 three	4 four
5 five	6 six	7 seven	8 eight
9 nine	10 ten	11 eleven	12 twelve
13 thirteen	14 fourteen	15 fifteen	16 sixteen

8

Can you point to all the numbers after 12?

What number comes after 19?

Can you point to number 21?

17 seventeen

18 eighteen

19 nineteen

20 twenty

21 twenty-one

22 twenty-two

23 twenty-three

24 twenty-four

25 twenty-five

26 twenty-six

27 twenty-seven

28 twenty-eight

29 twenty-nine

30 thirty

31 thirty-one

32 thirty-two

Shapes

Can you draw these shapes?

How many sides does a pentagon have?

What colour is the heart shape?

square

pentagon

right-angle triangle

cylinder

hexagon

cone

rectangle

cube

sphere

octagon

circle

oval

six-point star

heart

Which bear is stripy?

Patterns

What patterns are the bears wearing?

spots

tartan

checks

zigzag

wavy

stars

stripes

Which colour do you like best?

Where is gold?

Colours

Can you see all the blues?

red   orange   yellow   green   blue

Can you see all the yellows?

paintbox

silver

blue

12

Can you see the brushes?

Where is grey?

purple pink brown grey black

pen

white

brushes

yellow red

Can you see all the greens?

Can you see all the reds?

gold

13

Can you see the bumper?   Where is the bonnet?

Car

Are the headlights at the front or back of the car?

Where is the steering wheel?

What shape are the wheels?

roof

seat

rear window

back
light

bumper

wheel

door handle

Can you find the lights?

What colour is the car?

wing mirror

steering wheel

windscreen

windscreen wipers

front

bonnet

Can you see the windscreen wipers?

Where is the door handle?

door

headlight

WOB - ED 485

Body

face

arm

hand

head

hair

eyebrow

eye

elbow

nose

cheek

ear

chest

mouth

tummy

teeth

hip

lip

leg

chin

neck

knee

foot

16

What do you wear to bed?

What colour is the vest?

Clothes

Which boy has a stripy shirt?

How many children are wearing hats?

What colour is the boy's cap?

cap

shirt

vest

pyjamas

pants

slippers

dress

hat

shirt

socks

shoes

school uniform

bag

jumper

jeans

shorts

trainers

17

The house

Can you find these objects in your own home?

What colour is the telephone?

What time is it on the clock?

armchair

rug

phone

drawers

bookcase

book

cushion

computer

clock

sofa

18

Who's on the television?   **Which object rings?**

chimney   window   roof

wall

door   garage   gate

radio   houseplant   keys   newspapers

frames   television   MP3 player

Can you find some grass?　Where is the tree house?

The garden

Which object would you use to water plants?

Can you point to the birdhouse?

What colour is the rose?

rake

hand fork

rose

birdhouse

shears

flowerpot

watering can

bonfire

wheelbarrow

trowel

wellington boots

Can you find a trowel?　　What colour is the sky?

How many prongs are on the fork?

What colour is the wheelbarrow?

sky　　tree

tree house

bush

seat

wall

grass

flowers　　hedge

21

Good morning

What time do you wake up?

How many toothbrushes can you see?

sun

sponge

shampoo

toilet paper

soap

toothbrush

brushing your teeth

toothpaste

22

Where is the moon ?

What colour is the quilt?

Good night

When do you go to bed?

teddy

girl

What do you clean you face with?

bed

toilet

pillows

quilt

sleep-over

moon

What pattern is on the pillows?

story book

sleep

pyjamas

slippers

23

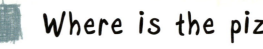

Can you find the steak?   Where is the pizza?

What we eat and drink

What is your favourite food?

What colour is the cheese?

milk

rice

cheese

boiled egg

bagel

biscuits

taco shells

Can you find the pancake?

cake

sweets

bread

Can you find the boiled egg?

strawberries

steak

scrambled eggs

turkey

salad

Can you see the turkey?

cheese and tomatoes on toast

seafood

pizza

pancake

burger

Can you point to a son?   Can you see a mother?

Family and friends

family   How many people are in your family?

Can you see a group of friends?

family

grandparents   sister   brother

father and son

mother and daughter

friends

26

School

What lessons do you take at school?

felt-tip pens

protractor

paint

set square

What can you use to measure things?

computer

pencils

ruler

exercise book

scissors

drawing

27

Fun and games

What is your favourite game?

Can you find things that bounce?

robot

football

drawing

puppet

basketball

cards

ABC

wooden blocks

bat

painting

How many girls are jumping?

jumping

model plane

climbing frame

28

What sports do you like?

chess

bubbles

tricycle

balloon

playing football

playing with dolls

robot car

cuddly toys

Can you see the roadworks? Where are the police?

In the street

What can you find in your street?

What colours are on the traffic light?

street lamp

hydrant

speed camera

telephone box

bin

railings

police

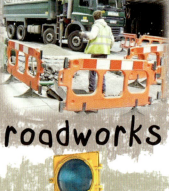
roadworks

recycling bin

statue

traffic light

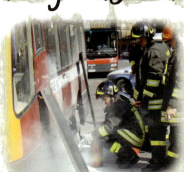
firemen

cash machine

Where are the firemen?   What colour is the hydrant?

Do you walk on the pavement or in the road?

How many different bins can you find? Can you find the telephone box?

tower

bridge

street lamp

window

car

building

pavement

tram

bollard

road

rail

31

What colour is the cooker? Where is the toaster?

In the kitchen

What do you use to stir things?

Can you point to the plates?

tinned food

jug

washing machine

tap

egg cup

toaster

bowl

tea towel

fridge

teapot

saucepan

cereal

Where is the cereal?

Can you find a kettle?

What can run hot and cold?

knife and fork

teacup

frying pan

What colour is the teapot?

whisk

cooker

iron

Can you find a bowl?

wooden spoon

ice-cream scoop

plates

kettle

Can you find a watermelon? Where is the orange?

Fruit

Can you point to the pineapple?

Can you see a pear?

bananas

apple

grapes

pineapple

lime

pear

kiwi fruit

Can you see an apple?

lemon

grapefuit

watermelon

peach

orange

tomato

strawberry

cherry

34

Vegetables

Can you find the carrots?

cauliflower

onion

broccoli

Where is the mushroom?

mushroom

turnip

potatoes

celery

pepper

runner beans

Can you see the potatoes?

sweetcorn

carrots

radishes

lettuce

Is a cygnet a baby swan?   Where is the fawn?

Baby animals

What is a baby horse called?

What is a baby dog called?

Can you find the bear cub?

kittens

ducklings

foal

calf

piglet

chicks

fawn

puppy

cygnet

lamb

bear cub

36

Which pet can fly?

What colour is the fish?

Pets

Do you have any pets?

rabbit

guinea pig

washing the dog

cat

dog

fish

parrot

tortoise

Does a tortoise move fast or slowly?

Can you find a cat?

By the sea

What do you use to see underwater?

Can you find a pair of sunglasses?

Can you find a lighthouse?

beach ball

paddling

spade

bucket

mask

waves

lighthouse

flippers

inflatable rings

windmill

swimming

deckchair

What can you dig with?

What number can you see on the fishing boat?

shell

crab

surfer

fishing boat

beach

sunglasses

What can you sit on?

On the farm

How many animals have two legs?

turkey

duck

donkey

wheat

crop

hen

ploughing a field

pig

horse shoe

pony

cow

Can you see the turkey?   Where is the horse shoe?

What colour is the cockerel's tail?

hay bale   sheep

barn

tractor

cockerel

goose

shire horses   goat   milk churn

Can you see the duck?

41

Can you find 5 hats?   Where are the sandwiches?

Party time

What colours are the balloons?

What colour is the wrapping paper?

balloons   sandwiches   silver bow   party hat

card   streamers

Can you find the tart?

gift tag

birthday cake   candle

Can you spot the clown? Where are the streamers?

How many orange presents can you spot?

Can you find two red noses?

presents

clown

tart

fruit salad

ice cream

wrapping paper

fruit juice   envelope

face paint

Mr. T Bear Esq
6 Bear House
Bearsville-Upon-Sea
BEARTUCKY
ABC 123

43

Can you spot the guitar?   Can you find a triangle?

Let's make music!

Which instrument has black and white keys?

Where are the bongos?

Can you see a tambourine?

flute

recorder

tambourine

saxophone

piano

guitar

banjo

microphone

bongos

triangle

violin

trumpet

French horn

44

Can you see 2 trombones?   Where are the bagpipes?

How many instruments have strings?

How many drums can you find?

bagpipes   drum   viola   trombone

musicians

Can you see the viola?

45

Wild animals

Where is the zebra?

Can you see an eagle?

How many animals have feathers?

How many animals have stripes?

Can you point to the giraffe?

crocodile

swan

panda

shark

wolf

cheetah

reindeer

crab

penguin

polar bear

hare

zebra

gorilla

46

Where is the camel?

Can you spot the wolf?

Can you see the crocodile?

Which animal has the longest neck?

owl

antelope

elephant

giraffe

fox

eagle

monkey

rhino

seal

snake

hippo

camel

dolphin

tiger

Can you see a crab?

Can you point to the train? Can you see the plane?

Let's go - on the move!

Which of these vehicles can travel on water?

Where is the skateboard?

Can you see a space shuttle?

train

balloon

boat

ocean liner

skateboard

motorbike

jet-ski

hovercraft

plane

ski-doo

raft

What colour is the car?

Which vehicle travels on snow?

lorry

bus

space shuttle

tram

bicycle

scooter

car

car

helicopter

Can you point to a hoverfly? Can you find the beetle?

Minibeasts

How many ants can you spot?

beetle

spider

frog

Can you find a grasshopper?

moth

fly

caterpillar

Which animals are slow?

worm

ladybird

bee

lizard

50

Where is the worm?

Can you find the butterfly?

Where are the 2 different spiders?

Can you see the caterpillar?

butterfly

snail

hoverfly

scorpion

ant

slug

wasps

grasshopper

Can you see the frog?

centipede

tarantula

dragonfly

51

What colour is the whale? Where is the tree?

I am big!

Can you find a yellow digger?

Can you point to the rocket?

Can you see an iceberg?

logging machine

crane

rocket

road roller

blue whale

tree

52

What has big ears?

Can you see the bison?

Where is the logging machine?

castle

bison

cargo ship

elephant

iceberg

airliner

digger

Where is the cargo ship?

Can you find the road roller?

Shopping

How many men are having haircuts?

Can you see the supermarket?

Where can you buy flowers?

cake shop

sweet shop

supermarket

art shop

cheese shop

barber shop

fabric shop

fish shop

delicatessen

flower shop

toy shop

music shop

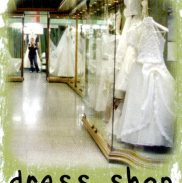
dress shop

Which shop sells cheese?   Where is the sweet shop?

Can you point to the oranges?

Can you spot the dress shop?

ASPARAGUS
3.90

RUNNER BEANS
5.90

GIANCARLO

greengrocer's shop

Can you find the hammer?   Where is the paint brush?

In the workshop

What colour is the oil can?

Where might you keep your tools?

Where are the nut and bolt?

screwdriver   pruners   paint brush   wrench

pliers   tape measure

oil can   plane

nut

bolt   trowel

61856

workshop

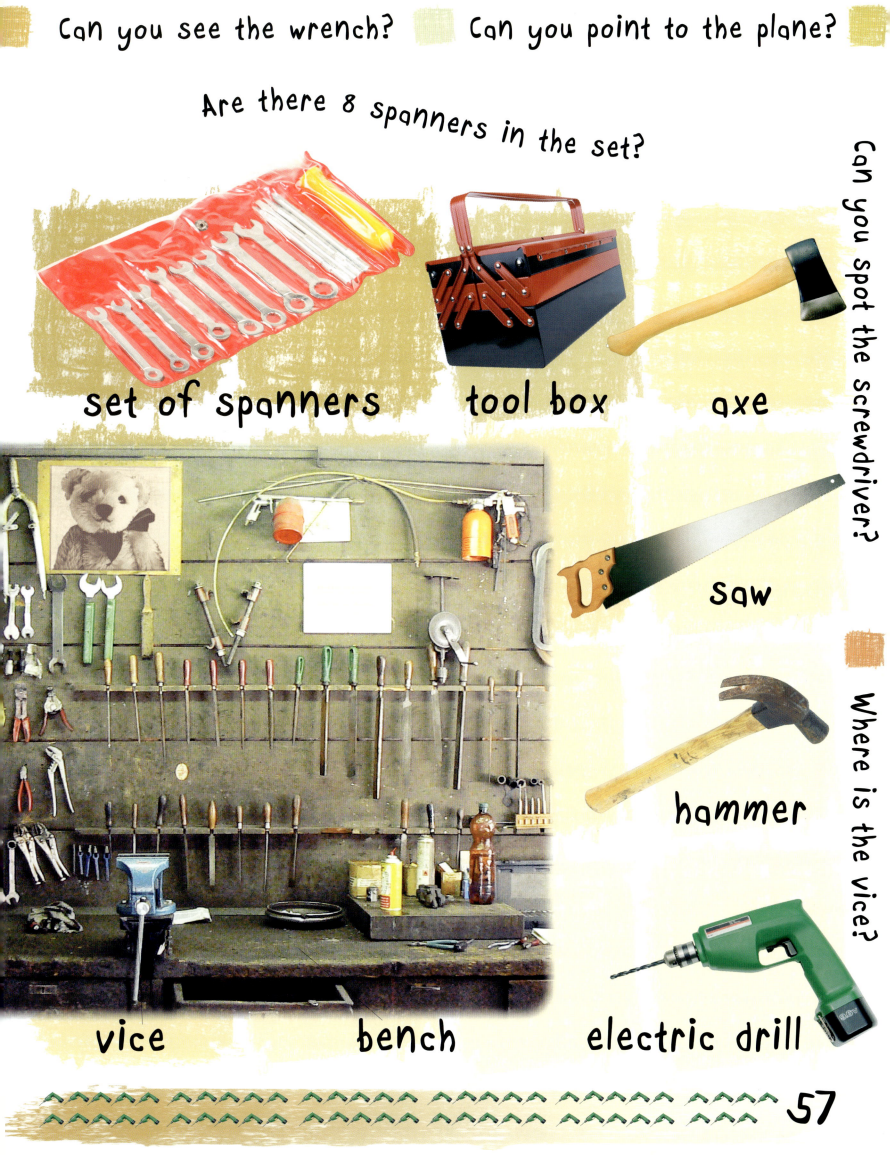

Can you see the wrench?   Can you point to the plane?

Are there 8 spanners in the set?

set of spanners   tool box   axe

Can you spot the screwdriver?

saw

hammer

Where is the vice?

vice   bench   electric drill

57

Out and about

Where would you go to catch a plane?

Where might you find lots of buildings?

Can you find 2 bridges?

mountain

waterfall

city

river

bridge

Where might you find lots of boats?

motorway

canal

airport

buildings

train station

lake

harbour

Where is the flood?

Can you see the fog?

Weather

Can you see the lightning?

Where is the tornado?

umbrella

hurricane

snow

Can you spot the rainbow?

tornado

lightning

raincoat

flood

rainbow

fog

60

Seasons

Which season is the coldest?

spring

summer

When is the sky blue?

autumn

winter

What follows winter?

Time

How many hours are there in a day?

When is home time?   What time is lunch?

night time

wake-up time

good morning

breakfast time

bed time

school time

bath time

lunch time

clock

tea time

play time

home time

lesson time

Index

How many words start with the letter E?

Index

How many words start with Q?
www.scribblersbooks.com
Can you find four words starting with V?
Can you find ...et?

Created, designed and edited by:
Elizabeth Branch
Stephen Haynes
David Stewart
Rob Walker
Mark Williams

ISBN-13: 978-1-905638-65-9 (HB)
ISBN-13: 978-1-905638-66-6 (PB)

Published in Great Britain 2007 by Scribblers, a division of Book House,
25 Marlborough Place,
Brighton
BN1 1UB

Telephone: 01273 603306
Facsimile: 01273 621619

A CIP catalogue record for this book is available from the British Library.

Printed and bound in Latvia.

A B C D
E F G
H I J K L
M N O P Q
R S T U V
W X Y Z